Trouble at the Pool

Jean Davidson and Lori Walker
Illustrations by Karl Edwards

Marco, Molly, Sam, Max & Annie

Copyright © 2020 Jean Davidson and Lori Walker

Illustrations copyright © 2020 Karl Edwards

All Rights Reserved.

ISBN: 978-0-578-66296-1

Printed in the United States of America

Published by The Davidson Yell and Tell Foundation, Inc.
P.O. Box 26706
Milwaukee, WI 53226
www.yellandtell.com

Trouble at the Pool
A Note to Parents and Teachers

The National Safety Council reports:

- Drowning accidents are the leading cause of death and injury of children under 5 years of age.

- Drowning is the second leading cause of injury-related death among children under the age of 15. (U.S. Centers for Disease Control and Prevention)

- More than 80% of drownings occur in backyard pools.

- Each year, 5000 children under the age of 14 are hospitalized for near-drowning events. Of these, as many as 20% suffer severe and permanent disabilities.

Always have a grownup watching children when they are near water!

To help improve pool safety, pool owners should have a 4-5 foot fence around the pool and a locking gate. Pool covers and pool alarms are also available.

All children should learn the 4 steps of Yell and Tell:

SEE IT……..FEEL IT……..YELL……..TELL

YELL AND TELL

SAFETY SERIES

LEARN what to do!
Book 5

Marco, Molly and Sam are playing at Molly's house.

"Hi, I'm Molly! I live next door. These are my friends, Sam and Marco."

"Oh look, the gate is open.
Let's go check out all the pool toys."

"He's the parrot from Yell and Tell.
He teaches children, if they see something dangerous,
to yell HELP and tell a grownup right away."

Feel it...

The kids feel scared. "What should we do? Let's use Yell and Tell!"

Max runs to get his Mom and Dad.
Marco and Sam yell, "HELP!" Molly yells, "Sit down, Annie!"

Tell!

"Mom, Dad, come quick! We need help! We were looking at the pool toys and I forgot to keep Annie with me."

Max's Dad is mad at Max and his new friends.

"The pool has a fence around it to keep children out! Even though the gate was open, you should not have gone inside!"

Remember the most important rule:

"YOU must always have a grownup watching you when you are near water!"

Squawk wants you to learn the 4 steps of Yell and Tell:

1. See it...
See something dangerous.

2. Feel it...
It's okay to feel scared, but then you need to take action.

3. Yell!
Yell "HELP!" as loud as you can.

4. Tell!
Tell someone right away.

Squawk, our mascot, teaches children to Yell and Tell.

Yell and Tell Heroes

In this story, Marco, Molly, Sam and Max are Yell and Tell Heroes. They yelled for HELP and told a grownup right away when they saw something that could be dangerous.

They each received their very own Yell and Tell certificate and Hero T-shirt.

Do YOU have a Hero story? Let Squawk know at www.yellandtell.com.
You will receive your own Yell and Tell certificate and Hero T-shirt.

Let's meet some other Yell and Tell heroes!

Mayor and Common Council honoring heroes from the community.

Ben, Alex, John, Cameron and Alec were playing on the playground and found hidden alcohol. They knew what to do because they had learned Yell and Tell. They reported what they found right away.

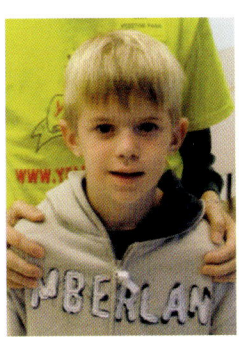

When Jared saw a little boy at the bottom of the pool at a party, he yelled and got help. When asked how he knew what to do, Jared said, "I just did what I learned in Yell and Tell at school!"

Anthony's friend fell through the ice at a cub scout outing. Anthony laid on the ice and held on to his friend's arm while yelling for help. He had learned Yell and Tell at school.

Eden's mother read her the Yell and Tell books. Eden yelled HELP when she saw a toddler running toward the road.

When his friend fell off a ladder, Kong yelled HELP to get his dad's attention. Kong had learned Yell and Tell at school.

The Fire Department honors Ryan for being a Yell and Tell hero. Ryan noticed a fire at the house next door and alerted his mom who called 911, and his father who ran next door and was able to save his eighty-one year-old neighbor.

Let's all sing the....
YELL & TELL SONG!

SEE IT   FEEL IT   WHAT SHOULD YOU DO?   YELL AND TELL LIKE SQUAWK SHOWS YOU!

TUNE TO T*WINKLE TWINKLE LITTLE STAR*. Words by Jean Davidson and Lori Walker.

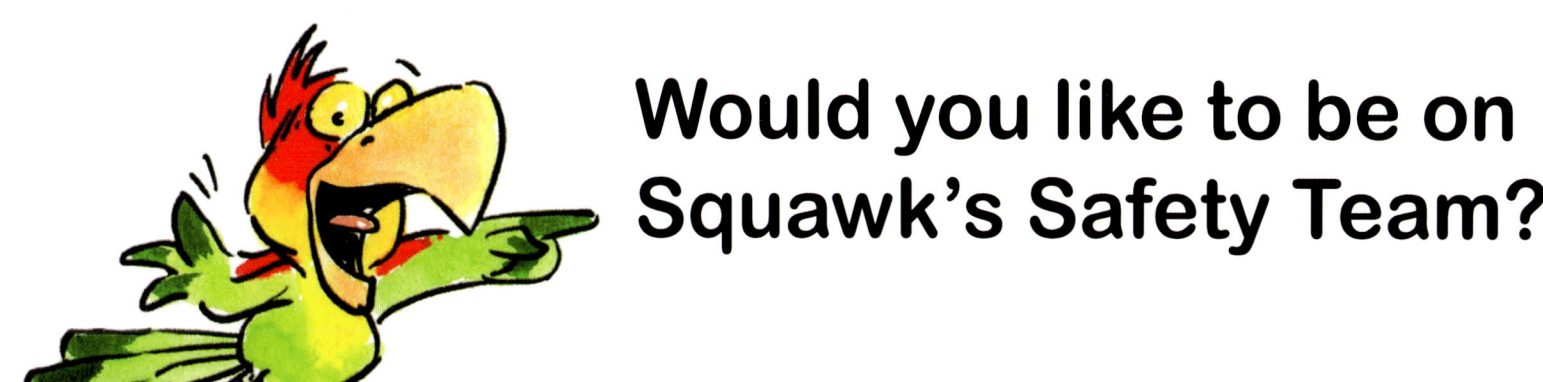

Would you like to be on Squawk's Safety Team?

Answer these questions to find out.

1. What are the four steps of Yell and Tell?

2. What word should you yell if you see something dangerous?

3. What do you do after you yell?

4. Why is it important to tell someone right away?

5. Can you think of other times you might need to Yell and Tell?

Share the Yell and Tell Safety Steps with your friends!

ANSWERS: 1. See it, Feel it, Yell, Tell. 2. Help. 3. Tell someone right away. 4. So help can come faster. 5. Someone playing with fire, someone about to drink poison, someone finding a gun, someone about to go off with someone they don't want to go with, and any time you see someone in trouble.

What is YELL AND TELL?

Yell and Tell is an easy-to-learn, interactive program. It is carefully designed to teach children the skills needed to take action if they see a dangerous situation.

YELL AND TELL'S FOUR-STEP PROGRAM:

1. SEE IT… – See a dangerous situation.

2. FEEL IT… – It's OK to be afraid, but then you need to take action.

3. YELL! – Yell HELP! to draw attention.

4. TELL! – Tell the nearest grownup.

Yell and Tell has developed programs for the following areas:

**POOLS - RIVERS/LAKES
FIRE - POISON - GUNS
CHILD ENTICEMENT - BULLYING
DRUGS AND ALCOHOL**

How can YOU help?

As a volunteer or donor, you can directly help bring the Yell and Tell program to more children.

- <u>Read</u> the Yell and Tell books and share the Yell and Tell four-step program.

- <u>Teach</u> Yell and Tell directly from our website. All teaching materials are free to download at www.yellandtell.com.

- <u>Download</u> our free App to reinforce these safety programs.

- <u>Donate Yell and Tell books and programs</u> to libraries, schools, child care centers, and other youth groups.

- Consider a <u>tax-deductible donation</u>, which will allow us to reach more children. Go to www.yellandtell.com.

Yell and Tell volunteers help bring the program to children everywhere.

Contact Us

For more information, contact Jean Davidson, Founder/Executive Director
(414) 771-9191
jean@jeandavidson.com
www.yellandtell.com

Yell and Tell
P.O. Box 26706
Milwaukee, WI 53226

A 501(c)(3) public benefit, nonprofit organization

<u>Like us on Facebook and follow us on Twitter @yellandtell</u>

Meet the Authors

Jean Davidson is the creator of the Yell and Tell Safety Program. She developed it after the tragic death of her four-year-old grandson, Ryder. Jean travels extensively introducing this life-saving program to children and adults. She is a long-time teacher and advocate of quality education. She is also an author who has written both adult and children's books. The Yell and Tell Safety books include: *Trouble at the Lake*, *Trouble at the Park*, *Trouble at the Playground*, *Trouble at the Party*, and now *Trouble at the Pool*. To see more, please visit www.yellandtell.com or www.jeandavidson.com.

Lori Walker is a children's librarian who encourages people of all ages to visit their local library. She has a master's degree in Educational Leadership and stays active in her community by making presentations for Yell and Tell. She also is an active master gardener. The loss of her nephew, Ryder, is the force behind her efforts to spread this safety program.

Meet the Illustrator

Karl Edwards has been illustrating children's books for over thirty-five years. He developed Squawk, the Yell and Tell mascot, and has illustrated all the books and educational materials for the Yell and Tell series in collaboration with Jean Davidson. Karl's illustrations appear in children's titles published by Random House, and his first author/illustrator book *Fly!* was acquired by Knopf. To see other examples of his work, please visit www.karledwards.com.

Dedication

Ryder Davidson Oeflein
(2002-2006)

Ryder was a four year-old boy who loved to run, jump, ski, and ride his bike.
One day, he and two neighbor boys went down to a creek filled with water. When the two younger boys fell into the water, the older boy became so frightened he didn't yell for help.
By the time an adult was alerted, only one of the boys was saved.

This book is dedicated to Ryder, who has inspired us to create and share the Yell and Tell program with children everywhere in hopes of preventing further tragedies.

J.D. and L.W.

Books from the Yell and Tell Safety Series

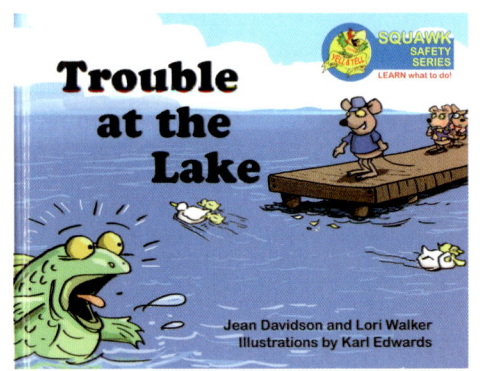

Marco, Molly and Sam were told not to play near the water. Trouble strikes when they go out on the dock to see some baby ducks. Simple text and vivid pictures help children learn safety skills that can save lives.

Marco, Molly and Sam go out to the playground at recess. They see someone getting bullied. Will they know what to do? Children will learn how to protect other kids and themselves when they see bullying.

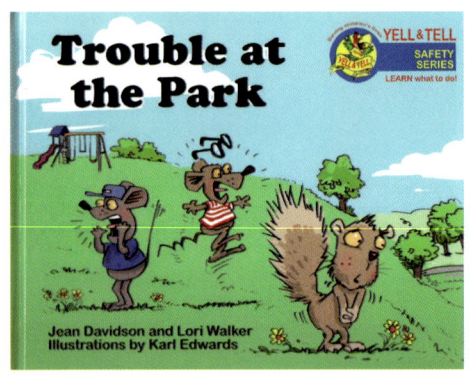

Marco, Molly and Sam know not to talk to strangers. But, what if a stranger invites Molly to go see some new puppies? Children will learn to see the signs of child enticement and what steps to take to help keep each other safe.

Marco and Molly are playing at Sam's house. They hear loud music and laughter coming from the basement. They sneak down and see teenagers having a party with beer and pills. Children will learn what to do when they see dangerous behavior.

When Max shows Marco, Molly and Sam his backyard pool, his little sister Annie gets into trouble. Children will learn what to do when they see trouble at the pool.

To order your own autographed copy, please go to www.yellandtell.com.
All proceeds will be used to reach more children.